The Curious Choice of Kina

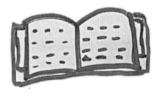

Samriddhi Mohanty

The Curious Choice of Kina

Kina is a girl who hates doing home-work
and is a TV lover.
She finds a way to escape her studies.
But it backfires. Do you think she can solve it?

Illustrated by – Samriddhi Mohanty

Acknowledgement

Special thanks to my mom
for finding my folder which had my story in it
and helping me in giving it a shape.

Huge thanks to my dad
for giving me creative ideas for the cover of the book.

Heartfelt thanks to my grade 1 teacher, Ms.Nicole,
for teaching me my grammer.

A huge thanks to all of you for picking up this book.

Once there was a girl whose name was Kina.
She never liked studying or reading books.

One day at school,

The teacher explained to her about the importance of taking responsibilities.
She asked her to do her homework on time.
But Kina didn't pay any heed to it.

In the evening Kina went back home
and crouched before the TV for a long long time.
She forgot everything her teacher had said.

Over dinner her mommy asked, "Kina, did you do your homework?"

Kina twitched her eyebrows, shrugged her shoulders and said,
"Yes Mommy!! I did do my homework."
And from that day onwards Kina started lying about her homework.

One morning Kina hatched a plan to escape studies.

She told her Mom in a pleasing tone,

"Mommy, I'm missing my Granny... I want to see her".

The next day Kina went away to her Granny's house.

Granny was very thrilled to see her sweetheart Kina.
She welcomed her with a fulfilling plate of food.

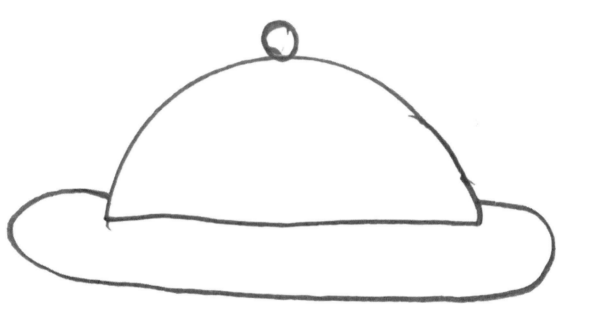

When Kina opened the cloche,
She was terribly shocked to see herself on the plate.

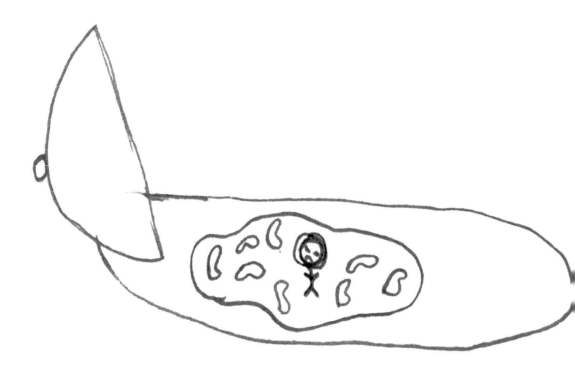

She was dumbstruck and began biting her nails.

She had turned into a small piece of bean lying on the plate.

Kina was horrified.

Then suddenly She saw herself as little as an ant sitting on the plate.
The ant-like Kina was screaming and trying to crawl out of the plate.

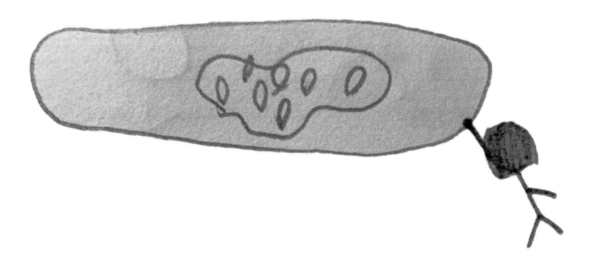

The ant-Kina was going on crying,

"Granny!! Gran!! How!!! Why did suddenly I shrink into a small Kina.
Why did I become such a puny insect?"

Her Granny said, "Kina my dearie!!! That's so simple.

You don't read!! You don't study at all!!

Your Knowledge can never grow. So you too can never grow!!!

You will keep on shrinking and shrinking till you become a tiny speck of dust.

One day you will disappear. One day you won't exist anymore."

*G*ranny continued,

"But if you promise not to run away from your responsibilities
Then magic will happen-
It's called the magic of Knowledge.
Slowly and steadily you will become that whole old Kina again."

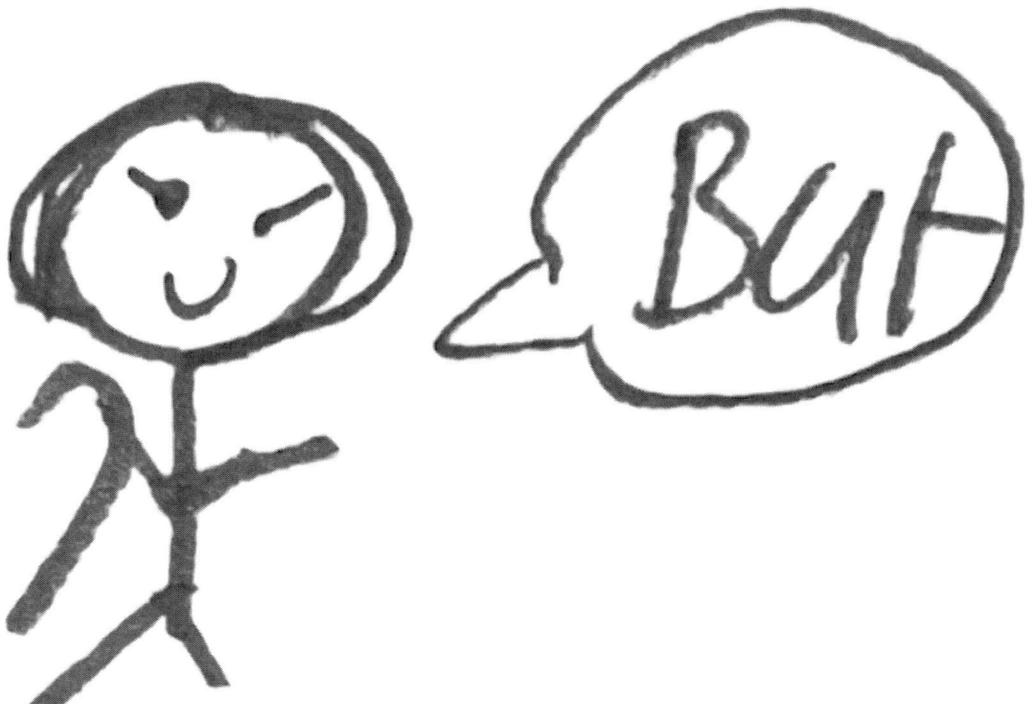
But

That's the moment when Kina woke up

And realized it was all but a dream.

Kina picked up a book lying beside her bed.

...that's how Kina made a choice.

About the Author

Samriddhi, fondly called as Simi,
is a student of Grade3
at Avondale Public School, Toronto.

She lives with her parents at North York, Toronto.

Simi's hobbies are
writing songs, short stories, craft, reading books & listening to music.
She is also passionate about gymnastics
and aspires to be a contortionist.

Get in touch with Samriddhi

repeateds@gmail.com

Printed in Great Britain
by Amazon

41501993R00016